Words To Love By

Words To Love By

Barbara J. Steele

authorHOUSE®

AuthorHouse™
1663 Liberty Drive
Bloomington, IN 47403
www.authorhouse.com
Phone: 1-800-839-8640

First published by AuthorHouse   07/07/2011

ISBN: 978-1-4634-2095-6 (sc)

Printed in the United States of America

Any people depicted in stock imagery provided by Thinkstock are models, and such images are being used for illustrative purposes only.
Certain stock imagery © Thinkstock.

This book is printed on acid-free paper.

POEMS AND SENTIMENTS
I HAVE WRITTEN OVER THE YEARS.

PEOPLE TELL ME THEIR THOUGHTS . . .
AND I EXPRESS THEM IN POETRY.
I DEDICATE THIS TO THOSE FRIENDS WHO
ALLOWED ME TO SHARE IN THEIR SADNESS,
JOYS, HOPES AND DREAMS.

THANK YOU

Barbara Steele
2011

I am dedicating this book to my five children,
Beth, Brenda, Diana, Dan and Darrin . . . .
and my thirteen grandchildren.

Welcome

I have tried to put the poems in categories to make it more user friendly. Most of my poems were written for a specific person or situation so there aren't any two alike. There will be similar phrases because I needed them to express a certain emotion I wanted to capture. If you are a true critic, I am sure you can find plenty of errors. I try to express the heartfelt feelings of the relative or friends of the person I am writing about.

In many situations I knew them personally and it was very emotional for me. We all know how difficult it is when we want to console someone . . . and we don't know what to say. I have found this to be my way of offering sympathy and joy. That is why I chose the title . . . WORDS TO LOVE BY.

I have not included last names and in some poems I may have changed first names. You will recognize the poem if I wrote one for you and I thank you for allowing me to be a small part of your life.

Patriotism

One Lone Soldier

He was a boy when the call went out
. . . for men to go to war,
The freedom he had always known
he could take for granted . . . no more.

Men and women . . . both young and old
were quick to answer the call,
They knew the danger they would face . . .
they were ready for it all.

The boy stood tall and said "good-bye"
as he tried to be so brave,
He knew that he would give his life
. . . if his loved ones could be safe.

He stands there looking at the sand
that has become his home,
The boy has now become a man . . .
he stands there all alone.

But we have not forgotten . . .
and we know God's by his side,
He stands among the bravest men
as he holds up freedom's light.

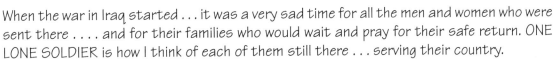

When the war in Iraq started . . . it was a very sad time for all the men and women who were sent there . . . . and for their families who would wait and pray for their safe return. ONE LONE SOLDIER is how I think of each of them still there . . . serving their country.

America's Tears

Breaking hearts, children crying . . .
mothers trying to be brave,
Thousands praying every day . . .
their loved ones would be saved.

A nation brought together by an evil
like no other, the bravery of
the fireman who will
die to save his brother.

How could You let this happen
. . . . is my prayer when I'm alone,
But evil isn't wrought by God . . . .
just men with hearts of stone.

So those of us who can . . . will hold
our children in our arms,
and promise them we'll never stop
protecting them from harm.

Raise up the flag and ask the Lord
for strength to see us through . . . .
Lest we forget those heroes
As we wave . . . Red, White and Blue.

This poem is dedicated to all the men and women who died on
September 11, 2001
and their families who must live with it every day.
The world can not . . . and must not . . . ever forget this tragedy.
I remember where I was that day . . . . do you?

Our Hero . . . . Our Son

We watch all the young men and women march by
in their uniforms, heads held high,
We're in awe of their poise as they head off
to war . . . to protect what they feel is right.

It's hard to believe that the handsome young
man there before us is going away,
For twenty-five years he has brought us such joy
and we feel such pride here today.

We, as his parents . . . . know he must do
what he feels is right in his heart,
We'll be right here waiting . . . for him to
return . . . as he feels he must now do his part.

So loved by his family . . . and dreams yet to come
. . . his future on hold for awhile,
The Mustang he'll get is just part of his plans
. . . as he shows you his beautiful smile.

We know God is with him . . . we pray every day
for our Bret to be back in our arms,
We know he is doing his best to succeed . . .
as he honors his country and home.

This was written for some friends of mine as they
were sending their son off to Iraq.
I am happy to say he was one who came home safely.

3

"Mac"

Who is this man we honor today . . .
He's a husband, a father and friend.
He was one of a kind . . . with a mind of his own
and he showed it . . . right to the end.

He married his sweetheart . . . the years would
fly by as they traveled through God's many trails,
How blessed they would be with five beautiful children..
It was faith . . . . that kept wind in their sails.

The one thing we know . . . was his love for his country
. . . . the Air Force was where he would shine,
He served in Korea with medals to show . . .
pride for country . . . would not fade with time.

He's remembered by many for coaching young
men . . . in the field of boxing . . . he loved,
Whether boxing or football . . . he gave it his all
. . . . it was one of God's gifts from above.

But life isn't easy . . . there were laughter and tears
. . . . health would suffer and soon take it's toll,
For a man who always took pride in his strength
. . . it was a powerful and crushing sad blow.

We all have our demons . . . so no one should judge
. . . . how would we do . . . if walking his mile . . .
If Heaven has lakes . . . I hope he's "casting" now . . .
no more pain . . . only love . . . and a smile.

Fred passed away Aug. 8, 2010. He will be very missed by
his children, family, friends who loved him,
but most of all by his loving wife, Carol.

Seven Lost

In years gone by . . . the world has seen
our country learn and grow,
The search for more space wisdom
led our astronauts to know.

The world was watching breathlessly
as seconds counted down . . . .
the graceful lift of metal as the
ship rose from the ground.

How thrilled they must have felt as
"lift-off" thrust them to the sky,
The ecstasy of what's to come . . . .
not fear . . . . or questions why.

With love and admiration we will pray
for these dear souls,
and try to understand that search for
science takes it's toll.

Their dreams and awesome bravery
will last in history,
God bless them as we know they
found their place in destiny.

Who will ever forget watching TV with such great
anticipation . . . and seeing the ship explode with
the seven astronauts on board?

January 28, 1986

Flags Waving In Heaven

We gather together . . . Harry's family and friends
as our hearts feel they're breaking in two,
We'll share happy stories . . . talk of good times he had . . .
as we know he would want us to do.

For sixty-four years he was married to Shirley,
his soul mate . . . . through laughter and tears,
His daughter and grandkids all made him so proud . . .
as he watched them grow up through the years.

A World War II veteran . . . . he never forgot . . .
. . . serving Patton . . . . what memories there,
No man loved his country with more pride than Bud.
He found joy on the Honor Flight earlier this year.

The years took their toll . . . but he never gave up . . .
while he could . . . he would sing favorite songs,
If ever you hear Tony Bennett's sweet voice . . .
. . . . you can bet Bud is singing along

We won't say good-bye . . . instead we say, thank you,
for bringing such love to our lives,
If the brave march in Heaven . . . Harry carries the flag
as he honors the fallen he joins.

Angels are singing . . . flags are all flying . . . .
as the veterans salute their dear friend,
It's so right Bud was taken on this Veteran's Day
. . . Standing straight . . . singing out . . . he is home.

⸻

Harry "Bud" died on Veteran's Day, Nov. 11, 2010
The twinkle in his eye was for great-granddaughter, Callie.
He'll be missed by all who loved him but especially his loving wife, Shirley.

Our Steve

We gather together . . . Steve's family and friends
as our hearts feel they're breaking in two,
We'll share happy stories . . . we'll wipe away tears
as we know Steve would want us to do.

A Vietnam Veteran . . . he marched with such pride
in parades and the funerals of friends,
And though he has left us . . . we'll never forget
. . . and the love that we feel will not end.

His marriage to Cindy brought joy to his life
as his soul-mate . . . through laughter and tears,
His sons and his grandkids all gave him such pride
as he watched and made plans through the years.

His birthday in June . . . saw him healthy and strong
as he walked his four miles every day,
Friday night at Friend's Circle was the one night a
week . . . he would smoke and have beer with his friends.

We won't say good-bye . . . instead we say thank you
for bringing such love to our lives,
If the brave march in Heaven . . . Steve carries the flag
as he honors the fallen he joins.

But some day . . . if you hear someone say . . .
"Good God Gertie", just look up and smile at Steve,
You can bet he is smiling and loving you too . . .
he would say . . . laugh with me . . . please don't grieve.

Grandpa Bill

Today we say good-bye to Bill . . .
the man who lived his life
always marching to his own drum
. . . . over eighty years in time.

He served in Pearl Harbor as
so many did that day,
His daughters brought him happiness
. . . . in such a special way.

He left his home when sister,
Margaret, needed him to come . . . .
How special is a brother's love . . . .
who's there to hold your hand.

For Toni, Mike and Jerry . . . .
it's a memory for life,
The comfort she received from Bill
was like a heavenly light.

He walked through life so quietly
and left us the same way,
We're thankful for the memories
we have to share today.

We love you.

2004

Children

KATHY

JASON

DEVYN

ANGEL WITH A BROKEN WING

DEAR GOD

ELIZABETH

It is always special to write for . . . or about children

This was a hard one for me to write. My friends called to tell me their
six year old daughter, Kathy, was in Iowa City, in the last stages of leukemia They asked
if I would write a poem for her when she went on to be with God

Kathy

Running, laughing, playing in the sun . . . we see our Kathy,
always thinking . . . planning . . . touching . . . all the little living things,
How she loves to cuddle puppies as they run around in circles . . . .
they . . . like Kathy . . . always moving . . . full of life and energy.

She grows quiet . . . not so often does she run or chase the kittens,
her little body tires . . . and moves slower as she plays,
Why, God, our little girl . . . why does she have to suffer so?
How we wonder at her strength as pain engulfs this little soul.

Now it's still . . . no more pain upon her tired little face,
Is that a smile . . . is God's hand reaching out to greet this precious child?
Could our little one . . . now free of hurt be that twinkling little star . . .
or that always present robin who's bright singing fills the air?

How much brighter are Your heavens, Lord, with Kathy's ringing laughter,
Maybe that will ease our sorrow as we know You take her home.
The joy and love she gave us will live on though years may pass,
Wrap Your gentle arms around her, Lord,
She's home with You at last.

Jason

If I could pick the time in life that brought me greatest joy,
I know the time would be when I first saw that "precious boy".
How do I tell you, Jason, of the happiness you bring . . . .
or how when I first held you . . . . I could hear the angels sing.

When I was very sick and felt I couldn't take the pain . . . .
your little hand in mine was like the touch of gentle rain.
I know you won't remember all the funny things we've done . . .
or the days we spent together playing games . . . . and having fun.

The day your Mommy said that you were going to move away,
I felt my heart would break but there was nothing I could say.
I wish I could be with you as you . . . . grow to be a man,
But if I can't . . . . just know I'm always here to take your hand.

There may be miles between us but I make this vow to you . . . .
Grandma's love will just get stronger and will always be with you.
Please don't forget me, Jason . . . or the time that we have shared,
Grandma loves you . . . . now and always . . . God Bless . . . and please take care.

I LOVE YOU . . . .
GRANDMA BARB

1985

When the grandmother asked me to write this she knew she had
cancer and might never see her grandson again. The mother was taking
him to Florida following a divorce. Barb died the following year and as
of 2010, Jason has never seen the poem. It sits in a frame at his uncle's.

Sweet Devyn

The tiniest of hands . . . the sweetest of smiles
. . . what a gift God presents us today,
Devyn entered this world in a faraway place
but it all put God's plan into play.

After months of deep prayer and our faith in
the future . . . we welcome this sweet little girl,
She joins her new family . . . with big brother, Jarrett,
She's a jewel . . . much more precious than pearl.

We'll all do our share to bring joy to her world
and to teach her the value of friends,
She'll learn that the family has love everlasting
. . . and the love of the Lord . . . never ends.

Thank you, Dear Devyn, . . . for bringing such joy
and great happiness . . . into our lives,
We pray that the angels will watch over you
. . . as their heavenly songs . . . fill the skies.

—◦◦◦—

This beautiful little girl came into our family as a baby
and she has been a blessing every day.

Angel With A Broken Wing

Molly . . . baby Molly . . . what a
precious gift you were,
God's angel with a broken wing . . .
He knew you'd find love here.

For thirty-three short days we got
to share our lives with you,
We tried to fix your broken wing . . .
but you were "passing through".

God wanted you to join His choir
of angels heaven bound,
And though you are not here today
. . . we feel you all around.

We'll think of you when a robin sings
so sweetly from a tree,
or when we hear a child laugh
at a puppy running free.

We know some day we'll be with you . . .
we'll hold you in our arms,
You'll play with sister Sarah . . . and
we'll know you're safe from harm.

You were a little butterfly
so fleetingly touched down,
Just time to touch our lives and hearts . . . .
then on to Jesus' arms.

This beautiful baby girl was born with a heart condition but
her parents considered the thirty-three days they had
her . . . a true blessing.

Dear God

Dear God, I hope you find me a home
with a mommy and daddy to love,
I'm not even born but I hear their voices
as they pray to You up above.

Please give me a mommy with a gentle touch
and patience with me when I cry,
And a daddy who will play with me . . . .
and just smile when I keep asking . . . why?

I know I'm going to cry a lot because
that is what babies do, but when
I get bigger . . . I will make them laugh
when they teach me to play "peek-a-boo".

I hope they will sing to me when I am
tired . . . and cuddle me when I am scared,
'cause I'm just a baby and everything's new
. . . and I'll have so much to learn.

We'll discover together what a family is
and I'll bring all the joy I can,
I know you will give me the best mom and dad
and to them . . . I'll give my tiny hand.

When Mommy smiles and makes me laugh
and Daddy makes me feel warm and safe,
I'll know you picked out the right ones for me
. . . and You found me the perfect place.

Amen . . . .
Baby Davis

Elizabeth

E   is for your beautiful EYES to see your mom and dad.

L   is for the LOVE you bring . . . and may you never be sad.

I   is for the INSIGHT God will give you as you grow.

Z   is for the ZEST for life that He will let you know.

A   is that you ALWAYS feel the joy we share today.

B   is for the BEAUTY you have brought to those who prayed.

E   is for ETERNAL life you'll learn to know in time.

T   is for the TRUST in God that you are going to find.

H   is for our Heavenly Father who watches over us all . . .
and blessed your mommy and daddy . . . with the most
precious angel of all.

Easter Sunday

Words Of Comfort

OUR DEAR ALLIE

THE OTHER SIDE OF HEAVEN
(VIC)

A MOTHER'S LOVE

JERRY . . . MY BROTHER

MY FRIEND . . . . JAN

TOGETHER AT LAST
(DON & JAN)

WHY I WROTE . . . OUR FRIEND BARB

OUR FRIEND BARB

KIRBY . . . EVERYONE'S FRIEND

OUR DAVE

JESSICA

MY LOVER . . . MY FRIEND
(BOB & MILLIE)

OUR LAURA

HELEN . . . LADY OF CLASS

GENE

JO MAMA . . . ANGEL OF MERCY

SWEET MAGGIE

BOBBY

WORDS OF COMFORT

SWEET TAMMIE

SHED NO TEARS

MARY LOU

ARBIE

DEAR STAN

Our Dear Allie

A beautiful lady . . . with love in her heart
she would meet every day . . . with a smile,
She loved a new challenge and faced it head on
. . . . to be sad was just not her style,

For eighty-three years she brought joy to so many
. . . as a mother, wife, painter and poet,
But her greatest joy was her love for the Lord
and her family . . . who she adored.

She could make you laugh . . . she would share your tears
whatever it was . . . . she was there,
. . . . She had the gift of making you feel
there was nothing . . . you couldn't bear.

Allie's passion for life was expressed in her paintings
. . . . her poetry mirrored her heart,
When God gave us Allie . . . He gave us much more
and she thanked Him through all forms of art.

But years took their toll . . . as we all know it will . . .
this dear lady grew tired and weary,
but she never gave up and still did her best
to be strong . . . and tried to be cheery.

But God must have felt it was her time to go
as He lifted her into His arms,
No more pain for this lady . . . her smile lights the Heavens
as she dons her best hat . . . . she is home.

———

Allie was one of those very special ladies you never forget.
She was spiritual, classy, kind, generous and a wonderful mother.
I feel very blessed to have been one of her many friends.

The Other Side Of Heaven

How lucky we were to have Vic in our lives
. . . the man with a smile in his heart,
He was there for his friends, for his soul mate, Irene
all the years . . . they were never apart.

He married his best friend . . . the love of his life . . .
they would share fifty-one precious years,
The Lord blessed their union with three loving sons
. . . as life goes . . . there would be joy and tears.

The deep love they shared gave them strength they
would need . . . as life handed them trials to bear,
They each lived with pain . . . but they never lost faith . . .
when they needed Him . . . God would be there.

As his health took a turn . . . he would never give up
. . . seven years . . . he would run in the Bix,
His true gift was singing . . . his voice can be heard
in the choir . . . as he now sings in Heaven.

I'm sure if we listen . . . we'll hear angels singing . . .
as Vic leads the great choir today,
He is now free of pain as he sings for us all . . .
our dear friend . . . from the far side of Heaven.

We thank You, Dear Lord, for the gift of our friend . . .
we were blessed to have Vic in our world,
If You wanted an angel . . . You picked the right man . . .
he earned wings . . . from his time here on earth.

Vic will be forever remembered by friends who loved him,
family who adored him and by his loving wife and best friend, Irene

A Mother's Love

A mother holds her newborn child
and looks into his eyes,
As years go by . . . he'll learn that
she is always on his side.

The day will come . . . he'll go to school,
his heart so filled with fear . . . .
She takes his hand and whispers . . . .
"not to worry . . . Mommy's here".

When he is grown . . . he'll go away
. . . begin life on his own,
The future always takes it's toll
. . . but love still brings him home.

The years have made her slower now
. . . it's hard for her to see,
But all she needs to make her smile
. . . is his voice . . . "Hey, Mom . . . it's me!"

If we could plan a perfect world . . . we
wouldn't lose our mother
For from the start . . . . we know that
she will love us like no other.

Today . . . she sings with angels . . .
and she dances free from pain . . .
Her love will live on in our hearts
. . . . until we meet again.

———❦———

This is for anyone who has lost a mother.

Jerry . . . . My Brother

When they were young . . . they lived to laugh,
. . . . the world was full of joy,
He always knew just what to say . . . .
this mischievous young boy.

The years went by and took their toll
. . . the laughter turned to tears,
That boy became a man and now
. . . his dreams had turned to fears.

We all face demons in our lives . . .
so who are we to judge . . .
This man who lived in pain for years . . .
who's family meant so much.

Please think of him with kindness
as he makes his journey home . . .
This father, son and brother . . .
never more to be alone.

⟨❦⟩

A man with a kind heart . . . is still missed every day.

My Friend . . . . Jan

We won't say good-bye . . . instead we say thank you
for years of shared laughter and tears,
How lucky we were to meet someone like you
who faced life . . . not discouraged by fears.

Your happiness came through your daughters and Don,
Your grandchildren were pure delight,
For those of us . . . who knew you as "friend" . . .
. . . our lives will be minus your light.

We won't say good-bye . . . because love will live on . . .
we'll see you in each gentle rain,
Each grandchild's laugh will remind us of you,
your compassion and love . . . without pain.

Our lives seem so empty but we know angels sing
as your laughter joins with those gone before,
We thank you, Dear Jan, for all that you gave . . .
Precious wife, mother, sister, daughter and friend.

Jan and Don were two of my oldest and dearest friends.
Jan was sick a short time before she went to be with The Lord.
Don was heartbroken and went to be with her just four years later.
He died of natural causes but those who knew him felt it was a broken heart.

Don And Jan
Together . . . . At Last

For the past four years . . . Don's life has been a
puzzle with the pieces . . . not seeming to fit,
He seemed to be searching for the main missing
part . . . that, of course, being Jan, his soul-mate.

We'll never forget his life as an athlete
. . . or how much he loved every sport,
His year with the Bronco's was one of his proudest
. . . but his ankles would cut that year short.

The year was a good one, despite that bad break
. . . since his marriage to Jan would begin,
It seemed clear to all of us . . . they fit just right
. . . . this would be a game they would win.

I like to remember their earlier years . . .
when they married . . . . and life was so fine,
Three beautiful daughters made years seem to fly
. . . . and the challenges faded with time.

In business . . . they had the respect of their peers
and the trust of their clients was earned,
But nothing meant more than the love of their girls
. . . with the laughter and joy to be learned.

I think Don would say . . . "please don't cry for me now",
as they walk . . . hand in hand . . . now together,
His prayers have been answered . . . what more can we ask
. . . than to be with our true love . . . forever.

Don left this earth to join his beloved wife, Jan, on Sept. 19, 2008. He will be deeply
missed by his loving daughters, family and friends who loved him.

Why I Wrote . . . . Our Friend—Barb

My dear friend, Barb, died of cancer after suffering for four years. Before she died . . . she asked me to write a poem for her . . . to be read at her funeral . . . . by me. I managed to finish it in time and she had me read it to her so she could hear it. She was having trouble talking by then . . . but she gave the "thumbs up" sign. Barb was known for her great sense of humor. She said if I didn't read the poem at her funeral . . . she would come back to haunt me.

As the casket was being rolled out of the church after the funeral . . . a jet flew over (quite low) and a friend of hers leaned over and whispered to me, "Leave it to Barb to leave in style". That was twenty-five years ago and she is still very missed by those who loved her.

Our Friend—Barb

Our lives are touched by many things that make us what we are . . .
through laughter and through tears we find our way.
And if we have God's blessing . . . we will find a special friend,
one like Barb who always knew . . . just what to say.

We talked about what "used to be". . . . when she was just a child,
the standing jokes with OLDER brother Bob",
The years went by and she became a mother and a wife,
Her life was full with three sons and her job.

Her ever changing future found her needing faith and strength,
She found this through the love of God and friends,
And time would heal the pain that comes to all . . . when love is lost,
The years would pass . . . and they remained good friends.

Her illness turned her life into a sea of growing pain . . .
but she handled it with humor and a smile,
She said "My grandson needs me so for Jason . . . I'll be strong".
How powerful . . . the love of a small child.

She knew what family love was . . . for they never let her down
Their support was like a beacon to the end,
And like us all there were regrets for things she couldn't change
but who are we to try . . . and judge a friend?

For fifty years our world was made a little brighter place,
Her presence brought such joy into our lives . . .
But now her pain has ended and her skies are blue again . . . .
The memories we have left . . . will long survive

Kirby . . . . Everyone's friend

When you think of Kirby . . . you think of his smile
and the joy he could find anywhere,
The ring of his laughter could always be heard
If you needed some help . . . . he was there.

He was a great Bears fan as everyone knew . . .
with Trisha and Tammy . . . he followed the Cubs,
They went to the games whenever they could
. . . for a "dad" . . . that meant sharing his love.

Golfing with some of his telephone buddies
on Sunday mornings was special,
Like fishing Lake Michigan . . . salmon, in mind,
to bring home . . . and just give to his friends.

He showed his faith in so many ways
and he never missed mass . . . . we all knew,
not even for sports would he take that time off
. . . . to his GOD he would always be true.

Two things he hated . . . baling hay and gardening
. . . . but he loved time with his Dad and Tim,
His love for his family was never in doubt
. . . their love was what mattered to him.

He knew Judy's job in the real estate world
meant late dinners and very long days,
But he never complained and was always right there
. . . He showed love . . . in so many ways.

This man that we knew as a golfer and friend
walks the beautiful greens that he loved,
his journey is over . . . . he found his way home . . . .
he found peace with the Lord up above

Our Dave

How lucky we were to have Dave in our lives
. . . to be blessed with the sound of his laugh,
Family and friends mourn the loss of his life
but the things we remember will last.

Dave's years here on earth seem so few to us all
but the memories he left will remain,
To Gina and Vince . . . he was big brother Dave,
. . . to Joan . . . he was such a good son.

Cousins and uncles shared the joys of his life
. . . racing cars, driving trucks, flying planes,
He was smart, he was gifted, he could fix anything
but he always found time to be kind.

So loved by his family . . . . so missed by the world
a friend who brought joy to our lives,
He brightened your day with a practical joke
if you're sad . . . he could still make you smile.

How thankful we are to have known this dear man
. . . to have been a small part of his life,
I'd like to think Heaven has cars to be fixed
where Dave and his dad make them right.

We won't say good-bye . . . instead we say thank you
for years of shared laughter and tears,
How lucky we were to know someone like you . . . .
who faced life with a smile . . . not with fear.

David left us to join his father, Gerald, in Heaven,
in 2006

Jessica

We know we are put on this earth for a reason
and we often ask . . . what could it be?
And why would someone as young as this lady,
Dear Jessica . . . now be set free.

We all have our problems, we try to
survive, as did she, in her twenty-nine years,
And we will not judge her . . . she is with God today
as He tenderly kisses her tears.

Her last days on earth, filled with laughter and
joy as she played with the sons she adored,
Alexander and Austin were her greatest blessings
and may be the reason she was born.

Some day they will ask why their mother is gone
and they'll hear of the love they were given,
But God needed someone with laughter and love
. . . a lady to brighten the Heavens.

Some day we will all leave our loved ones
on earth . . . and like Jessica . . . there will be tears,
I'm sure if she could . . . she would say please don't
cry . . . I'm with God . . . I'm at peace and I'm free

Jessica adored her sons and cuddling them was one
of her greatest joys.

My Lover . . . My Friend

I wasn't even looking when
this gift was sent to me,
This gentle man who's smile
lights up the room.
I thought God had forgotten
all my tears and silent prayers,
but He waited . . . . for the
perfect man for me.

The years have flown so swiftly
. . . it just seems like yesterday,
You still light up my world
with just a touch.
We laugh at silly things we say
. . . we cry at children's pain,
We hold each other . . . .
when it seems too much.

But God has yet another plan . . . .
He wants to call you home,
He gave us twenty-six bright
years to share,
Just hold me, my dear husband,
my lover . . . my best friend . . .
Remember . . . you're the answer
to my prayers..

For Bob and Millie
Two of the bravest people I know.
October 17, 2003

Our Laura

"Don't cry for me", is what she'd say
if Laura was with us today,
"I have felt your love as you felt my pain
as you knelt by my side . . . to pray.

Be glad for this dear lady . . . that her pain
has found it's end,
Now God has called her home and
holds her gently . . . like a friend.

Her years on earth were few but what she
left will long survive,
Her love . . . her smile . . . her laughter
. . . found their way into our lives.

The love she shared with Curt was what
God wanted love to be,
Patience . . . love . . . and trust
was what they showed their family.

To know her . . . was to love her . . .
and time can't take that away,
How blessed we were to share her world
. . . the beauty of her days.

The joy and love she gave us
will live on though years may pass,
Wrap Your gentle arms around her, Lord,
she's home with You at last.

Laura will be forever remembered and missed by
friends who loved her, children and grandchildren who adored her,
And by her loving husband and best friend, Curt.

Lady of Class

Who is this lady we're talking about?
She's the mother of T.J. and Fred,
A native of Milan . . . . her days would be spent
with dear Charles . . . the man she would wed.

Their marriage was blessed with two loving
sons . . . . and together they worked on the farm,
She dearly loved flowers . . . her favorite . . . the rose . . .
would be seen in her care of the yard.

The years would go by and her love for her family
would show in her gift as a mother,
This hard working woman . . . found time for the games
. . . and her cheering . . . much louder than others.

She loved golf and bowling . . . but nothing meant more
than her boys . . . and the time they would share,
When leaving the house . . . she would look like a million
. . . . Her cooking . . . the best anywhere.

But time took it's toll . . . as we all know it will . . .
This dear lady grew tired and weary,
She never gave up and she still did her best
To be strong . . . . and tried to be cheery.

But God must have felt it was her time to
go as He lifted her into His arms,
Together at last . . . Charles and Helen . . . are home
. . . as they stroll through God's heavenly farm.

Helen, 90
Helen will be forever remembered and missed by
friends who loved her, family who adored her . . .
and most of all by her loving sons . . .
Fred and Tom

Gene

Christmas Day may seem a very sad time . . .
for someone to leave us on earth,
But think of the joy and the singing of angels
. . . .as they celebrate dear Jesus birth.

Our hearts will be sad as we miss our
kind friend . . . but it's joyful . . . we really should be,
The bonds of his illness and physical pain . . .
have been lifted . . . he's finally set free.

The man we remember would work every day
. . . his smile was known to us all,
His care for his clients was easy to see
. . . since they still ask for him when they call.

His love for his family was such a strong gift..
. . . the kind we respect and admire,
They returned it each day as they cared for his
needs . . . their compassion and love never tired.

He tried to be strong and he fought to the end
. . . but God felt it was time to go home,
Today he stands straight . . . as he greets . . . dear
old friends . . . our Gene . . . is never alone.

We won't say good-bye . . . instead we say thank you
for years of shared laughter and love,
His journey is over . . . he found his way home
. . . .he found peace with the Lord up above.

—————

Gene left us to join God on
December 25

Jo Mama.... Angel of Mercy

A beautiful lady . . . with heart of gold
and a smile to light up the room,
She touched lives of thousands in so many ways
as they learned her compassion was true.

Fifty short years ago . . . . Jo married Dave . . . .
her soul-mate and best friend for life,
Their love brought them daughters, three lovely girls,
who were there when she fought her last fight.

Emergency Medical Services grew . . . . with her
teaching of mercy and love,
Ask eight hundred firefighters . . . and nurses alike
. . . . if this angel was sent from above.

The first there to help when the need would arise
Jo was honest . . . and straight to the point,
she lived life to the fullest . . . and treasured each day
she would share . . . as a mother and wife.

So loved as a grandma with stories to tell and her
laughter as she spread her joy,
A grandma who leaves scores of memories strong
by a lady so loved by us all.

God must have felt it was her time to rest . . . .
as He brought her home . . . to His arms,
If angels have wings . . . . I'm sure Jo has earned hers,
Our Angel of Mercy is home.

———◆———

Jo was known as "Mother of EMS", Emergency Medical Services.
She was loved and honored by everyone who knew her.

Sweet Maggie

Who is this lady we honor today . . . .
a mother and wife with true class,
For ninety-two years she brought joy to us all
. . . . and the wisdom she taught us . . . . will last.

At the young age of twenty . . . she married her
soul-mate . . . the friend and companion she loved,
For sixty-two years they would farm the land . . . .
and raise three loving children . . . from God.

The years found her busy . . . her hands never still . . .
her crocheting and scrap books . . . still here,
She kept many pictures of family and friends
. . . . for those memories she always held dear.

Years would fly by . . . they found new things to do
. . . Jim and Maggie found joy everywhere,
They liked the casinos and visiting friends . . . .
they brought laughter and fun they would share.

But life isn't easy . . . and there would be tears
as Jim went on to be with the Lord,
She showed us her strength and her faith every day
in her sweet little smile . . . . kind and warm.

God must have felt it was her time to go
as He lifted her into His arms,
Together at last . . . . Jim and Maggie . . . . join hands
. . . as they stroll through God's heavenly land.

Bobby

He talked about "What used to be",
when he was just a boy . . . .
the family that he loved with all his heart,
His music was a gift that he was
blessed with very young . . . and he gave
us fun and music from the start.

His Grandma was his biggest fan . . . . he's
with her now today . . . . I'm sure
his friends and family gather round,
His voice is loud and clear . . . and the angels
join him as he sings "Lord . . . This time
You Gave Me A Mountain" . . . .
but I'm strong.

His years on earth were few . . . but what
he left will long survive,
His love, his smile, his music
will live on. He lived life to the fullest
and he'd say "Don't cry for me,
Go find your favorite fishin" hole . . .
That's where I'd want to be.

If there's a country band in Heaven, I'm sure Bobby is
playing the lead guitar.

2004

Sweet Tammie

Sweet Tammie had a loving heart
. . . . for any friend in need,
She had a gift for turning tears to smiles,
The joy she brought was shared
with all the people that she knew,
If they needed her . . . she'd
walk that extra mile.

Her illness turned her life into
a sea of growing pain . . . .
but she handled it with grace and dignity,
The love she had for Tim would give her
strength to see it through . . .
as they faced this road together
. . . . hand in hand.

She saw her share of sadness in
her few short years on earth,
How glad we are . . . we got to be a part.
This daughter . . . mother . . . sister . . . friend
and sweetheart will live on . . . .
for we'll carry her forever in our hearts.

Shed No Tears

When your heart is filled with sadness
and you try to understand,
Just remember all the good times
with this very kind young man.

Though the time we had to know him
went so swiftly . . . too few years,
I am sure if Mike could speak to us
. . . he'd begin with "Don't shed tears".

Dry your eyes, Mom, just be glad
the things I feared . . . are now behind,
All the love of those who cared . . . .
could not release my troubled mind.

Please forgive me for not being there
to share the coming years,
I love you . . . but at last I rest . . . .
I ask . . . . shed no more tears".

———

This young man took his own life on his 20th birthday.
Drugs had put demons in his mind that he couldn't get rid of.
He loved his mother very much and I think this is what he
would have wanted to say, if he could.

1983

Mary Lou

Why her, you ask as sorrow fills
your heart and clouds your mind,
your friends who offer love . . . trust that
relief will come with time.

Be glad for this dear lady . . . that
her pain has found it's end,
Now God has called her home and
holds her gently like a friend.

She made the lives around her
so much happier and gay,
Her family knows she loved them
in a very special way.

Her years on earth were few but
what she left will long survive,
Her love, her smile, her laughter . . . .
found their way into our lives.

The love she shared with Gene was
what God wanted love to be,
Patience, love and trust
was what they taught their family.

To know her was to love her
and time can't take that away,
How Blessed we were to share
her world . . . and the beauty of her days,

The sky may seem much bluer
and the stars may seem too bright,
If they do . . . it's Mary Lou . . .
who's found her place in Heaven's light.

Arbie

"Don't cry for me . . . . I'm finally at peace..
the world I last knew has passed on,
I now fish and golf in *God's* heavenly hills
..the fear and the pain are all gone."

I think if he could . . . that is what he would say
to his family and friends gathered round,
To Willie, his angel, who stayed by his side
who knew every sigh . . . . every sound.

The years and his health took a toll on this man
but the memories of him will remain,
We'll think of his smile . . . and all of his charm
and the humor he showed every day.

This strong man we knew as a golfer and friend
walks the beautiful greens that he loved,
His journey is over . . . he found his way home . . .
He found peace with the Lord up above.

———

He will be remembered and missed by his family
and friends who loved him, and most of all by
his loving wife, Willie.

Dear Stan

How lucky we were to have Stan in our lives
. . . to be blessed with the sound of his laugh,
Family and friends mourn the loss of his life
but the things we remember . . . . will last.

For sixty-one years, with Hazel, his soul-mate
. . . . he lived life with zest and true joy,
He served in the army with honor and pride
All his life . . . he showed strength of a boy.

A loyal employee . . . he gave work his "all" . . .
but his family was still his true love,
A son and two daughters were his pride and joy
and he knew they were sent from above.

His passion for life was his gift to the world . . .
one his family and friends will remember . . . .
Whether golfing the greens . . . or fishing the lakes
..he showed deep, caring love . . . . for all nature.

The angels are singing in beautiful harmony
as Stan joins their heavenly chain,
How can we be sad . . . when at last he's found
peace and his body is free of all pain.

We won't say good-bye . . . instead we say . . . thank you
for years of shared laughter and tears,
How blessed we all were to know someone like Stan
who faced life with a smile . . . . not with fear.

Celebrations Of Life

ANGELS OF MERCY

TOGETHER . . . . FOREVER
(WEDDING)

WHAT IS SHE . . . TO ME?

OUR FRIEND . . . TIM

OUR FAMILY MAN
(TOM)

I LOVE YOU MORE
(LAURA)

MAKE A DIFFERENCE
(GRADUATION)

BROTHER . . . DAVID

FRED
(BIRTHDAY)

YOUR BIG DAY
(BILL)

COACH GLEN

MY MOTHER
(JANET)

HUSBAND-FATHER-FRIEND
(JIM)

CHRISTMAS MEMORIES

IT'S REALLY OK

MY GIFT

TOMORROW
CELEBRATIONS OF LIFE

SENIOR OLYMPIANS

THE MEANING OF LOVE
(WEDDING)

MANY FACES

FIFTY GOLDEN YEARS

TRUE FRIENDSHIP
(CAROL AND TED)

GENE . . . OUR FRIEND

WHO IS MARY

I HEAR YOU
(KEN)

DEAR GENE

MY FRIEND . . . CAROL

OUR FRIENDS ADVENTURE
(WILSON'S)

A MOTHER'S HEART

THANKS FOR THE MEMORY
(ALLEMAN REUNION)

I AM SO BLESSED

THE END

Angels Of Mercy

Angels of mercy is what you are called
. . . and how worthy you are of the name,
People who know of the "Alzheimer world"
learn to deal with the fear and the pain.

You hear the same questions and see people
cry as they search for someone they might know,
Their world has grown smaller . . . they can't
find their way . . . wandering the halls, to and fro.

You are the foundation these patients will know
as their memories fade in the night,
I speak for the families who mourn for their loss
and trust you to help in this fight.

Your caring and love are the caregiver's gift
and we thank you for all that you do,
We trust you with loved ones who need special
care . . . we pray God will be there for you.

Don't lose your patience . . . we know it is hard
. . . as you work many hours every day,
Please help save their dignity . . . just be their friend
. . . . we ask God to show you the way.

This is a dedication to caregivers everywhere . . . who have
committed their hearts, their time and their skills in order to ease
those last days . . . in the sunset . . . of many lives.

Together . . . . Forever

Jerrod and Tiffany join hands on this day
to begin their journey of marriage,
Each challenge they meet will add strength to
their love . . . . and the memories they will now carry.

Friends since seventh grade . . . years have
flown by . . . . but the best is yet to begin,
From the beginning . . . Tiffany loved his sweet smile
And Jerrod knew that Tiff was for him.

The Illinois Army National Guard is a big part
of Jerrod's life now . . . and will be until he returns,
But Tiffany and Kailyn will be here to greet him
. . . . as their life as a "family" begins.

It's easy to see what a great "dad" he'll be . . . as he
teaches . . . and spends time with Kailyn,
There's no greater gift a grandparent can ask
. . . . than a loving stepfather to protect them.

We all have our faults but your love will endure
. . . as you stand by the one you adore,
The hand that you hold at your wedding today
is the hand you will hold evermore.

Heaven is ringing with angels sweet singing
As your family and friends share your love,
We wish you the best as your future unfolds
and we join God's blessings above.

＊＊＊

Joined in marriage
2008

What Is She—To Me?

To some . . . she is the lady with
the smile at the store,
To others . . . she directs the choir
and makes their voices soar.

Her children know her love is
endless . . . always there to give,
The church sees that devotion is
the way she wants to live.

Her husband knows when times are hard . . .
she'll back him all the way,
And when we need encouragement . . .
she'll find the words to say.

For Mabel . . . she is always there to
lend a helping hand,
We wonder at her energy and strength
at every stand.

But Mariellen knows that she is
blessed with God's great love,
How fortunate are we to share
her sunshine from above.

The world is far much happier
a place for us to be,
But I am even luckier . . . .
for what is she to me?
She is my sister.

———❦———

Our Friend . . . . Tim

How lucky we are to have worked with Tim . . .
a man with a smile and a heart,
No matter what job you might happen to have
. . . you feel part of his team from the start.

But "working" is only a part of this man
. . . a part we were happy to share,
The love of his life is his family and friends,
and he's never too busy to "care".

Another new chapter begins for you now
. . . we wish you the best . . . though we're sad,
You'll be in our hearts and we'll never forget
. . . as a leader . . . you're the best we have had.

You have a great gift but it's nothing that's learned
. . . it's called character, wisdom and charm,
We'll think of you often . . . you'll be missed every day
. . . . our best wishes are sent from the heart.

How lucky the people who will work with you now
as you greet every day with a smile,
Don't forget us, dear Tim, as you leave us today . . .
. . . . you've earned love and respect from us all.

Tim, my friend and supervisor, went on to a new job. He will
be very missed but his new employees will be lucky to have him.
June 18, 2010

Family Man

You're one of a kind . . . you're one in a million
you're one of the "good guys" . . . . it's true,
We all know your family is tops on your list . . . .
you're the "Captain" in charge of that crew.

You could write a book . . . of adventures you've had
. . . . like hopping a train headed west,
The songs you recorded are full of such hope . . .
in your heart . . . . you would reach for the best.

Your time in Korea was not always bad . . . .
like the time you were driving your "leader",
He said he would drive . . . since you kept dozing off
. . . you were lucky he didn't demote you!

You've always loved sports . . . you held records in pole-vault
. . . for ten years . . . you coached Milan baseball,
You always find time for events of the grand-kids
still . . . you're happy to referee football.

We still don't know why, when you were a boy,
you would stick your finger in sockets,
That may be why thunderstorms . . . still entertain you
but I think that's a whole different chapter.

You make us laugh . . . you make us smile . . .
you are there to dry all our tears,
You're a very loved man who brings joy to our world
. . . . we can't wait for the next sixty years.

HAPPY 60th BIRTHDAY, TOM

I Love You More

Dear beautiful lady, co-worker and friend,
you're one in a million . . . we know,
You light up the room with your beautiful smile
. . . and you keep everyone on their toes.

You're one of the few who could hold down
two jobs . . . and be a success . . . doing each,
Emily and Kate were priority "ONE" . . . .
and next . . . . your desire to teach.

You're one of our "family", the Mel Foster Crew
. . . and nothing will ever change that,
Your life is a lesson on how to stay strong
. . . . your motto . . . is NEVER GIVE UP.

You set an example for every new agent . . . .
you can do anything . . . with hard work,
And now you can take time to be "Grandma Laura",
spend time with your daughters and Curt.

God had a plan when He made us all friends
as He knew there were things we would learn,
We hope you'll come often . . . your desk will be here,
And we hope you will still call this "home".

It's easy to see that your love was well spent
. . . . as your daughters adore you today,
And Curt shows his love as he stands strong
beside you . . . . you are loved . . . in so many ways.

This beautiful, young woman was my co-worker when she was stricken with Lou Gehrig's Disease. She continued to work as long as she could and she came to the office as often as possible. She was often greeted by, "I love you, Laura". In her last days of coming in . . . the only words she would say were, "I love you more". I'm sure none of us will ever hear that phrase without thinking of our dear Laura.

Make A Difference

Brenda Sue . . . I can't tell you the joy that you bring
. . . or the pride that I feel here today,
Since the day you were born and were laid in my arms
. . . . your future was headed this way.

Your smile lights the room . . . your love is a gift
to the people you have in your life,
Your children are blessed with your patience
and laughter . . . . and two loving arms in the night.

You dealt with your pain and we all saw your strength
as we watched you accomplish your goals,
Your students will learn that you never give up . . .
and you don't let bad breaks take their toll.

The world at your fingertips . . . future so bright,
as you and Shawn walk hand in hand,
Your beautiful children to guide as they grow
. . . you're a blessing to family and friends.

Your heart of gold . . . so full of life . . .
the desire to teach what is free . . .
Go into the world . . . make a difference today
. . . as you have to your family . . . and me

Love,
Mom

Brother . . . David

When you were just a little guy . . .
you filled our home with joy,
Behind that quiet little smile
. . . was a mischievous little boy.

But you grew up to be a fine young
man . . . and went away to school,
The beginning of a full new life
when you found your true love, Sue.

You married and found life in Texas
. . . . to be where you would stand,
Though we would miss you every day
. . . it was part of God's great plan.

When you were blessed with two sweet
boys . . . . it seemed life was complete,
A job you liked, a wonderful wife . . . .
what more was there to need?

You found there was one more great
joy . . . . when Jordan would be born,
Life held a whole new meaning
when you held him in your arms.

There may be miles between us . . .
but you're always in our hearts,
Just know you're always very loved
and we're never far apart.

—◄●►—

Happy Birthday David
We love you . . . .
Your sisters

Fred

It's that time again . . . .
for the "Man of the Year" . . .
the man who will never be old,
He's a loving husband, wonderful brother,
a son any mother would love.

He's busy with hunting and fishing
all year . . . we never get tired of his tales,
the quack of a duck . . . or honk of a goose,
He's also been seen shooting quail.

Whether napping at noon . . . .
or "putting out fires" . . . . he's still
at the top of his game,
He's the dearest of friends and he's
loved by us all . . . . he's the man who makes
sun . . . out of rain.

———

HAPPY BIRTHDAY FRED

From your friends at
Rock Island Mel Foster Co.
2007

Your Big Day

When you were just a little guy . . .
you didn't have a care,
You didn't know what life would bring
. . . or what would get you there.

As you grew up . . . became a man
. . . you thought of future plans,
The beginning of a full new life . . .
when you found your love . . . Luanne

It seemed life was complete when you were
blessed with two sweet boys,
Bret and Brandon filled your home
with happiness and joy . . . .

How proud you should be feeling . . .
as you've moved up all the way,
You drove a truck for many years . . .
you're the president today.

You make it fun for everyone . . .
no matter what you do,
It might be watching Nascar . . .
or Las Vegas . . . calling you.

We hope you know how much you're
loved . . . by friends and family,
That's why your birthday means so much
to all of us today.

——————

Happy Birthday Bill

Coach Glen

If you're lucky . . . you've heard the stories of Glen . . .
the adventures and great escapades,
He's the only one here who has ordered his lunch . . .
from a gas pump . . . . and then raced away.

Now . . . that's not so bad . . . but my favorite of all
was the time he broke into a house,
He was showing the home to some clients of his . . . .
but the problem . . . he showed the wrong house (not for sale).

Did you know he can sing? . . . . Dolly Parton's his best
imitation of great western queens,
He gives it his "all" . . . but it's easy to see . . .
he doesn't sing well . . . on his knees.

He's leaving us now for his real true love . . .
the kids he has coached all his life,
He'll be missed by us here . . .
but he's "king" on the field . . . .
Lucky kids . . . to have Glen show the way.

April 17, 2007

Glen was one of my co-workers at the Rock Island Mel Foster office.
This was for his retirement party and his friends know that what I
have described about our friend . . . really happened. He made us
laugh for years and we loved him. He went on to be the
baseball coach at Rockridge . . . .
Good job, Glen!!!

My Mother

My beautiful Mother . . .
the words seem too few,
to thank you for all of the
kind things you do.

I've watched through the years
as you deal with each day,
. . . . no matter what happens . . . .
you find time to pray.

For fifty sweet years . . . .
you have been a good wife,
Your devotion to family
always done with a smile.

The words of your doctor . . . .
describe you so well,
"A remarkable woman",
with stories to tell.

Your friends know you'll
be there . . . . if ever they call,
They know you're a "treasure"
. . . and loved by us all.

Gene loves to tell how
he asked for "my hand",
But Dad made him nervous . . . .
he asked you . . . . you said "yes".

You adore your great-grandsons
. . . . children's laughter is free,
You're God's gift to many . . . .
But especially . . . to me.

Happy 75th Birthday

54

Jim
Husband . . . . Father . . . . Best Friend

It's hard to believe you are seventy-five . . . .
you're the youngest in spirit we know,
You're the man we all go to when we need a friend . . .
. . . . we have learned over time . . . . your love grows.

You can turn tears to laughter . . . . and fear into joy
. . . . it's a gift we have all come to treasure,
Your love for your family is easy to see . . . .
what they feel in return . . . can't be measured.

Your marriage to Janet was just the beginning . . .
of many bright years and adventures . . . .
The birth of your daughter was part of God's plan
. . . the gift of Deb's love . . . a great chapter.

It still makes us laugh to remember that Gene
was afraid to ask you for Deb's hand,
In fear of your answer . . . he chose to ask "Mom",
who could see Deb had found a good man.

Life isn't all blue skies and laughter . . . it's true
. . . there have been some struggles and tears,
but you've always been there with compassion so
strong . . . .in your arms you would drive away fears.

You'll have many stories to tell the great-grandkids
. . . . watching them grow . . . . is such fun,
For Janet . . . the words she treasures the most
are . . . . "My dear . . . . you are still number one".

HAPPY 75th BIRTHDAY May 10, 2008
There aren't enough words to thank you for all you do.
We love you!

Christmas Memories

I tried to think of something special for this Christmas day
to tell you what you mean to me in . . . Oh . . . so many ways,
There must be more to Christmas than the presents we can buy,
I think back many years . . . and all the holidays gone by.

I still see all the little faces peeking down the stairs . . .
wondering if it's really true . . . that Santa has been there!
At first you heard soft whispers . . . as if not to miss a thing . . .
your eyes . . . all bright reflections of the tree and pretty things.

But most of all . . . I think of all the laughter and the joy . . .
The moment filled with precious love . . . for every boy and girl,
And now you're on another journey making dreams come true
. . . . always finding ways to turn the gray skies into blue.

And one day you will look upon a tiny, trusting face . . .
You'll have so much to tell him . . . how to win . . . and lose a race,
My heart is filled with happiness . . . my tears . . . are tears of joy
. . . I thank you for my memories . . . not bought with any toy.

Love . . . . Mom

It's Really Ok

It's a beautiful day and I'm so blessed
. . . who says it's hard to get old?
The memories I still dream about . . .
are too precious to never be told.

There's no reason to fret if the kids don't call
. . . they have busy lives of their own,
and "independence" is what we taught
. . . as we sent them down life's rocky road.

My friends still call and I have my health
. . . that's more than many can say,
So it's okay if the kids don't call
. . . they love me anyway.

I know they realize I'm here . . . .
and my love for them is strong,
There's nothing they could ever do
to make me feel I'm wrong.

I sit here looking at the stars . . . .
knowing how lucky I am,
It's really not bad . . . being alone
. . . but WAIT . . . . I think it's my phone!

My Gift

The greatest gift we can ask for in life
is the love of our family and friends,
The time that we spend sharing laughter
and joy . . . is the gift we hope never ends.

But life isn't simple and tears come with
years . . . . the people we love go away,
We don't understand why God's plan isn't ours
. . . . but we know that He hears when we pray.

The children we're blessed with . . . put stars in the
sky . . . and rainbows to brighten sad days,
But if they must leave us . . . we know angels sing
as they help us to wipe tears away.

We met once again after years had gone by . . .
you brought fun and laughter to me,
Together we talk of the sorrow we've known
and the blessing that friends seem to be.

We look all our lives for someone we can trust
. . . someone who is honest and true,
How lucky and blessed I have been in my life
. . . and the greatest gift . . . having met you.

Sometimes the greatest gift is that special person you happen to meet.

Tomorrow

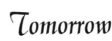

The world is full of challenges
that some will never try,
In years to come . . . they'll try to
think of all the reasons why.

"It can't be done" . . . they'll tell you
as you try to find your way,
"The times are hard and you will fail",
is what you'll hear them say.

But those are just the losers
who will never be on top,
They look for reasons to give up
and are always first to stop.

Be thankful for the faith you found
to make it on your own,
The world is yours . . . if you will try
. . . just know you're not alone.

If yesterday seemed hopeless
don't let fear control your life,
Have faith in what you're doing . . . .
Through the darkness . . . you'll see light.

Never give up your dreams.

Senior Olympians

How lucky we are . . . we still want to compete
. . . . to do things we've not done before,
What does it matter if we try and fail . . . .
we aren't doing it just for the score.

We've learned through the years that the
prize isn't gold, it's the smile on a little child's face,
It's the touch of a baby's hand gently in yours
or a teen as she runs her first race.

We've seen wars before and we've cried many tears
but we know love and faith will prevail,
Each in our own way shows the heart of a lion
to attempt . . . means never to fail.

Life isn't behind us because we are gray . . .
the love we still feel . . . ever strong,
The gifts that we offer are service and smiles,
the days of compassion are long.

We greet each new day with the hope of a child
. . . that decisions we make will be right,
We're blessed with our memories and visions to come
. . . as we take on this challenge . . . called life.

The Meaning Of Love

David and Becky join hands on this day
to begin their great journey together,
Each challenge they meet . . . will add strength
to their love . . . as they promise to love . . . forever.

A very wise lady once answered my question . . .
"What does falling in love really mean?"
Her answer was simple . . . I share it with you
. . . as you start to fulfill all your dreams.

When the one that you love . . . puts her heart
in your hands . . . hold it gently and softly . . . with care,
For if you should drop it . . . or squeeze it too hard
. . . it will wither . . . and dissolve into air.

But treat it with love . . . and speak sweetly and softly
of hopes that you share here today,
That heart will grow bigger . . . and stronger with time . . .
and the hard times will just fade away.

Your marriage is all part of God's master plan . . .
as you share with the children . . . this gift,
May your home fill with laughter as memories are made
. . . may compassion help dry away tears.

Heaven is ringing with angels sweet singing . . . .
as your family and friends share your love,
We wish you the best . . . as your future unfolds . . .
and we join God's blessings above.

———◄═►———

David, Becky and family were united in marriage
On April 24, 2010

Many Faces

A man of many faces is the way we all see Tom
.... and the reason he is everybody's friend,
He tells it like it is ... in his soft and knowing voice,
never known to just be following a trend.

Tom's well-known as a mentor for his patience and kind
words ... he teaches that the honest way is best,
He won't lie just to sell a house, his moral ground is strong ...
he will show them that each day is just a test.

To know him means you get to hear his tales of the past
and you understand what makes this man so dear,
Of course, he isn't perfect ... and he doesn't try to be ...
... but he makes it fun ... just to have him near.

Nancy and his family are his true loves here on earth
.... it's clear to everyone he's ever known,
We also know his Faith is what sustains him through day
... his love of God has made him ever strong.

He'll make you laugh ... he'll make you cry ... with a twinkle in his eye
somehow ... he seems to know just what you need,
How blessed our lives have been to know this very special man ...
his new chapter has begun .... with God to lead.

This man of many faces ... known as husband, dad and friend ...
can begin to live his life .... without the stress,
The door is always open ... you are always welcome here ....
Our dear friend .... to us all .... you are the best.

—◆—

TOM
HAPPY RETIREMENT FROM YOUR MFC FRIENDS
Dec. 7, 2009

Fifty Golden Years

Memories sweeter as time passes by . . . .
. . . how golden the years they have shared,
They count all their blessings . . . remember their
dreams . . . and it's clear to us all . . . they still care.

When Al thinks of Ruth . . . the love of his life,
he knows she's the girl of his dreams,
They met long ago . . . just young kids you
might think . . . but they planted their love as a seed.

When Ruth first met Al . . . her heart was all his . . .
his gentleness showed her the way,
Their home was then blessed with four loving children
. . . what more could they ask . . . you might say.

Alvin's years with John Deere were a strong base to
build on . . . they worked to complete all their plans,
Through laughter and tears . . . the years have flown by
. . . while they greet every day with a prayer.

They stand here before us . . . with memories strong
. . . . their hearts filled with joy and love,
They still love to dance . . . joined by family and friends
. . . . who rejoice with the angels above.

HAPPY ANNIVERSARY

Alvin and Ruth Celebrated their 50th Wedding Anniversary
December 28th, 2007

Dear Carol True Friendship

How blessed we are to have special
friends that we may not see every day,
But the sound of their voice or greeting each time
. . . . warms your heart in it's own special way.

Carol handles each challenge that comes to her now
with the strength that has always been there,
We can all learn a lesson from Carol and Ted
. . . . that each problem is less . . . . when it's shared.

We wish you the best in this season of joy
and we want to remind you . . . . we're here,
Whatever you need . . . just give us a call . . .
your friends, who all love you . . . . are near.

Get well, our dear Carol, you're missed every day
in this season of carols and cheer,
we pray every day for your healthy return
God is holding you close . . . . do not fear.

We love you.
This was written for our co-worker who happened to be having
health issues and was very missed by everyone. I am
happy to say she returned to work and she is fine.

Gene . . . Our Friend

The best gift in life is a special friend . . .
. . . . one who always knows just what to say,
He quietly walks into everyone's life . . . .
with a twinkling eye . . . goes on his way.

He starts every day as he writes in his book . . .
. . . he knows that is one of the "rules".
He's always considered . . . the strong-silent type
. . . and his humor is one of his tools.

Don't try to upset him . . . he won't take the bait,
. . . he learned long ago how that works,
You may hear him mumble while walking away
. . . that he doesn't have time for the jerks.

If you look for perfection . . . you won't find it here
. . . he doesn't pretend to be that,
He's dependable, honest and won't let you down,
he's a man that will keep you on track.

The best in the business and known for years
. . . his honesty trademarks his life,
But everyone knows that his family comes first
and the love that he shares with his wife.

He's a gentleman, agent, co-worker and friend . . .
it must be quite clear who we mean,
He's the man we all miss and think of each day . . .
He's a treasure to us . . . our dear Gene.

Who Is Mary

She's the lady who can make you smile
with just a few short words,
She sees the beauty in the sky . . . .
or in a tiny bird.

She's little but she's mighty
and she has a heart of gold . . . .
I'm sure there are so very
. . . many stories to be told.

The beauty of the falling snow
brings joy to all who see,
But no one brings the calm
and peace . . . that Mary does to me.
She is my friend.

Mary was one of our co-workers in our
Rock Island Mel Foster Co. office. She always
Liked my poems but she asked if she would have to die
To get one. Of course, I wrote this just for fun.
To know Mary . . . was to love her.

2003

I Hear You

My eyes are closed . . . I'm very tired
. . . my family's all around,
I feel as though I'm spanning time
. . . my feet won't touch the ground.

There is no pain except for what
I know you're feeling now,
I want to say "Don't cry for me
. . . tears aren't what I'm about".

I hear your prayers and feel the love
your voices send my heart,
I'm fighting for each breath I take
. . . that we won't have to part.

Please, know whatever happens . . . .
it is part of God's great plan,
And who are we to question Him
Who holds us in His hands?

I pray you'll hold each other close
and laugh at memories,
Don't ever doubt the love we share . . .
and please don't cry for me.

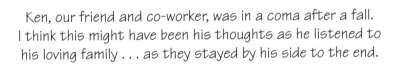

Ken, our friend and co-worker, was in a coma after a fall.
I think this might have been his thoughts as he listened to
his loving family . . . as they stayed by his side to the end.

Dear Gene

It doesn't matter how long you've
been gone . . . you're thought of every day,
You're one of those people we never forget
. . . no matter how long you're away.

Your clients still call asking only for you
. . . they say you're the only one they will trust,
We try to explain you left orders to follow
. . . with honesty . . . being a MUST.

New agents don't realize how much they miss
from the knowledge you have and could tell,
They have to just settle for stories of clients
who called you to buy or to sell.

You have a great gift but it's nothing that's
learned . . . it's called character, wisdom and charm,
You're thought of so often . . . and missed every day
. . . our best wishes are sent from the heart.

We wait for the day you will come through
the door with your smile and thought for the day,
Until then . . . we pray for your health to return . . .
you are missed . . . more than we can say.

This wonderful gentleman has been out of the office due to
health problems . . . but we pray he will be able to return soon.
We miss you, Gene.

Our Friends Adventure

Another adventure for Kathy and Lew
as they pack up to head down the road,
They've proven that life is a challenge to take
and they laugh as they finish each load.

You give it your "all" . . . and hope for the best
. . . . there's no guarantee in the end,
If you're lucky, you're blessed with a partner you
love . . . as for Kathy and Lew . . . . their best friend.

With every dream . . . there are chances to take
and lessons to learn on the way,
Life is too short to let fear hold you back
or to worry what someone might say.

You know we will miss all the Hi's and the Lo's
and the singing that greets every day,
Your generous hearts make you loved everywhere
. . . and we'll miss you the very same way.

Your long list of friends will continue to grow
as you head back to places you've been,
Please know you'll be welcome . . . . we hope you'll
come back . . . . and we hope we're on that list of friends.

From all your friends at Mel Foster Co.
Rock Island, IL

A Mother's Heart

A mother's love is special
which only she can give,
Always searching for your good points
. . . . always willing to forgive.

A mother's touch is gentle . . .
releasing all your pain,
To help you see the good times
. . . . forget the days of rain.

A mother's voice is tender
to sooth your troubled fears,
To make the monsters of the night
. . . . like darkness . . . . disappear.

A mother's song is sweetness . . . .
that's sung throughout the year,
It glows with warmth and honesty
. . . . it's love and endless cheer.

A mother's love is priceless . . .
a gift that grows each day,
It carries with it pride and trust
. . . . more than words can say.

This is the only poem in the book not written by me.
My daughter, Brenda, wrote it for me many years ago.
It is one of my favorites.

Luther Heights

I wanted a safe and secure place to live . . . .
when a friend said . . . . try Luther Heights,
I called and was greeted by such a sweet lady
. . . it was Sandy . . . and I felt this was right.

It felt warm and friendly as I walked through the halls
and met some of the men and the ladies,
With people who care . . . . like Sandy and Tony . . . .
I felt there . . . I could live out my days.

For Sandy and Chuck . . . the days are so busy . . .
as having four children will do,
Now the kids are all grown but she cares for us here
and her kind heart still carries her through.

So thank you, dear Sandy, for all that you do . . .
as you smooth ruffled feathers each day . . . .
It's because of your patience and bright, cheerful smile
that the folks here . . . are happy to stay

Merry Christmas 2010

This was written as a fun song for the 60th ALLEMAN Class Reunion in 2010. If you are from that era, you are familiar with the Bob Hope theme song . . . . Thanks For The Memory. The verses are written about that class and, hopefully, brought back a lot of memories for everyone.

THANKS FOR THE MEMORY
The time we spent together . . . the years we were apart
We did our best to leave our mark . . . we did it from the heart . . .
How lovely it was . . . .

THANKS FOR THE MEMORY
Of football records made . . . the fight to make the grades
We named the colors green and white . . . gave Pioneer's their name
How perfect it was . . .

Many's the time that we fasted
Oh, well . . . it was swell while it lasted
We followed the rules, one by one
We did have fun and no harm done . . .

THANKS FOR THE MEMORY
It doesn't seem like sixty years . . . we had our graduation
But here we are . . . close friends again . . . to share this celebration . . .
So thank you so much . . .

THANKS FOR THE MEMORY
Of those who have passed on . . . we feel their love today . . .
I think they'd say . . . "Have one for me" . . . so lift your glass and say . . .
How lovely it was . . .

We said goodbye with a highball . . .
But we managed to stay out of trouble . . .
But we were intelligent people
No tears, no fuss, Hooray! For us . . .

SO THANKS FOR THE MEMORY
Forget about the little dreams that never did come true . . .
Awfully glad I met you, cheerio, and toodle-oo . . . .
I thank you so much . . .

I Am So Blessed

So often . . . I think of the places I've been
and the people I've met through the years,
I've laughed and I've loved . . . and found many friends
and, of course, we have shed many tears.

But that doesn't matter . . . for everyone has . . .
each challenge . . . . will just makes us strong,
Don't sit and complain . . . that won't fix a thing . . .
to give up . . . would make it so wrong.

I worked at Mel Foster for eight happy years
where I met friends I'll have all my life,
To name just a few . . . I can call Jane or Cindi . . . .
any time of the day or the night.

Deb is the lady of soft-spoken words we could
count on to always be there,
We've gone our own way . . . but the bond . . . keeps
us close . . . we all have our stories to share.

It's closeness like this that remind us each day
of the reasons . . . . friends play such a part,
time won't change a thing because nothing means more
. . . than those friendships . . . so dear to my heart.

Thank you, my friends, for the beautiful memories
And the comfort you have been through the years.

Dear Reader

I hope you were able to find some enjoyment in the poems you have just read. Each one was written from words expressed to me by a loved one or family member. This was just a few of the many I have written over the years. Thank you for taking the time to read this . . . and I hope you were able to feel the love that went into each one. I heard someone say . . .

"Scars remind us of where we've been . . . they don't have to remind us of where we're going".

THE END